# SALTWATER AQUARIUM SECRETS

## Expert Tips for Thriving Reef Tanks and Coral

Nhyira Adzo

# Table of Contents

# INTRODUCTION

The world of saltwater aquariums is an awe-inspiring realm where vibrant coral reefs, exotic fish, and stunning marine life come together to create an underwater paradise in your own home. However, achieving this marine wonderland requires more than just filling a tank with water and fish. To truly thrive, a saltwater aquarium demands careful planning, dedication, and knowledge of the delicate balance that sustains life beneath the waves.

In Saltwater Aquarium Secrets: A Guide to Reef Tanks, Fish, and Coral Care, you'll uncover the essential steps to setting up and maintaining a healthy and beautiful reef tank. Whether you're a beginner excited about diving into the world of saltwater aquariums or a seasoned aquarist looking to enhance your knowledge, this guide will provide you with invaluable insights into everything from tank setup and water chemistry to fish species and coral care. We'll explore the fascinating art of creating a reef ecosystem that supports the vibrant life within it. Along the way, you'll learn how to carefully choose fish and corals that not only complement each other but also thrive together in harmony. With practical tips, expert advice, and a deeper understanding of the marine world, you'll be equipped to create an aquarium that will be both a source of joy and pride for years to come. So, whether you're captivated by the colors of corals or mesmerized by the graceful movement of fish, this guide will be your essential companion on your journey to creating the ultimate saltwater aquarium. Let's dive in!

## WELCOME TO THE WORLD OF SALTWATER AQUARIUMS

Step into a world of wonder and beauty—where vibrant coral reefs, exotic fish, and thriving marine life come together to create a stunning underwater ecosystem right in your home. Saltwater aquariums offer a unique and captivating way to bring the ocean's magic into your living space. However, as enchanting as they are, these aquariums also require a deeper level of care and attention to detail than freshwater tanks.

In this guide, you'll discover everything you need to know to embark on your journey into the world of saltwater aquariums. From setting up the perfect reef tank to selecting the ideal fish and corals, we'll cover the essentials to ensure your aquarium not only looks beautiful but also supports a healthy and sustainable marine environment. As you learn the fundamentals of saltwater aquarium care, you'll soon realize that it's more than just a hobby—it's an art. Creating a thriving reef tank involves understanding water chemistry, maintaining the right balance of nutrients, and carefully selecting compatible species that will thrive together in your tank.

Whether you're a beginner or a seasoned aquarist, this guide will provide you with the knowledge and tools to create your own breathtaking marine paradise. So, dive in and get ready to explore the vibrant and fascinating world of saltwater aquariums!

## THE JOYS AND CHALLENGES OF REEF TANKS

Reef tanks are some of the most beautiful and dynamic aquariums you can create, offering a window into the stunning underwater world of coral reefs. The vibrant colors, diverse marine life, and intricate ecosystems make reef tanks a captivating addition to any home. However, the journey to creating and maintaining a successful reef tank is both rewarding and challenging.

# THE JOYS OF REEF TANKS

1. Natural Beauty: A well-maintained reef tank can transform your space, providing a living, breathing piece of art. The rich colors of corals, the graceful movements of fish, and the interplay of light and water create a mesmerizing display that brings the wonders of the ocean into your home.

2. Biodiversity: Reef tanks support a diverse array of marine life, from delicate corals to colorful fish and invertebrates. Watching this complex ecosystem thrive is incredibly fulfilling, especially as you learn more about each species' unique needs and behaviors.

3. Educational Experience: Maintaining a reef tank offers a hands-on education in marine biology, chemistry, and environmental science. You'll gain a deeper understanding of how marine ecosystems function, as well as how to create a

sustainable environment that mimics the natural ocean habitat.

4. Sense of Accomplishment: The satisfaction of seeing your reef tank flourish is unparalleled. The delicate balance required to keep everything healthy—from water quality to fish compatibility—can be challenging, but when it all comes together, it's an incredibly rewarding experience.

## THE CHALLENGES OF REEF TANKS

1. Complex Setup and Maintenance: Reef tanks require a higher level of attention compared to freshwater aquariums. Setting up a reef tank involves not just choosing the right fish and corals, but also understanding water parameters such as salinity, pH, temperature, and calcium levels. Regular maintenance, including water changes, equipment upkeep, and monitoring

water quality, is essential to keeping the tank thriving.

2. Cost: Starting a reef tank can be a significant investment. High-quality equipment, such as protein skimmers, filtration systems, lighting, and heaters, can be expensive. Additionally, the cost of corals, live rock, and fish can add up quickly. However, the long-term rewards often justify the initial investment.

3. Fragile Ecosystem: Reef tanks are sensitive environments, and small changes can have big impacts. Corals and fish rely on a delicate balance of nutrients, water parameters, and compatible species. If something goes wrong—whether it's a spike in ammonia levels or a compatibility issue between tank mates—it can affect the entire system.

4. Patience and Time: A reef tank takes time to develop and stabilize. It's not uncommon for

beginners to experience setbacks, such as algae blooms or coral stress, as the tank matures. Successful reef keeping requires patience, learning from mistakes, and understanding that it can take months, or even years, to achieve the fully balanced ecosystem you envision. Despite these challenges, the rewards of a reef tank are immense. With the right knowledge, equipment, and care, the joy of watching your reef tank flourish will make every effort worthwhile. Embrace the learning process, and soon you'll experience the true magic of having your own piece of the ocean at home.

## WHAT YOU WILL LEARN IN THIS GUIDE

This guide is designed to equip you with everything you need to know about setting up, maintaining, and enjoying a thriving saltwater reef aquarium. Whether you are a beginner taking your first steps into the world of saltwater tanks or an experienced hobbyist looking to refine your skills, you'll find valuable insights and practical tips to help you succeed. Here's what you can expect to learn:

1. Setting Up Your Reef Tank

We'll walk you through the essential steps of setting up your reef aquarium, from choosing the right tank size and equipment to properly preparing your environment for marine life. You'll learn how to set up filtration systems, lighting, heaters, and other critical components, ensuring that your tank is ready for its first residents.

2. Understanding Water Chemistry

Water quality is key to the health of your reef tank, and this guide will help you understand the essential parameters—such as salinity, pH, alkalinity, calcium, and nitrate levels—that need to be balanced. You'll learn how to test, monitor, and adjust these factors to create a stable and healthy environment for your corals and fish.

3. Choosing the Right Fish and Corals

Selecting compatible fish and corals is one of the most exciting aspects of reef tank ownership, but it also requires careful planning. You'll learn how to choose species that will thrive together, how to introduce new inhabitants to your tank, and how to avoid common mistakes like overcrowding or introducing incompatible species.

4. Caring for Corals and Marine Life

Proper care of your reef tank's inhabitants is critical for their well-being. This guide will cover the basics of feeding, acclimating, and maintaining the health of corals, fish, and invertebrates. You'll also learn how to troubleshoot common health issues, such as disease or stress, and how to prevent potential problems before they arise.

5. Tank Maintenance and Long-Term Care

Reef tanks require ongoing maintenance to stay in top shape. You'll learn the best practices for performing water changes, cleaning filters, maintaining equipment, and monitoring the health of your reef tank over time. This section will provide tips on establishing a routine to ensure your tank remains a thriving, balanced ecosystem for years to come.

6. Troubleshooting and Problem Solving

Even the most experienced aquarists encounter challenges. This guide will teach you how to identify and address common reef tank problems, from water quality issues to pest control, algae blooms, and more. You'll gain the confidence to solve problems and keep your tank in optimal condition.

7. Advanced Reef Keeping Techniques

For those looking to take their reef tank to the next level, we'll cover more advanced topics like fragging corals, propagating species, and maintaining delicate ecosystems like SPS (Small Polyp Stony) and LPS (Large Polyp Stony) corals. This section will help you become an expert in reef tank care. By the end of this guide, you'll have a deep understanding of how to create and maintain a beautiful, healthy reef aquarium. Whether you aim to create a peaceful fish-only tank, a stunning coral garden, or a full-scale reef ecosystem, you'll be well-prepared to bring your vision to life and enjoy the countless rewards of reef tank ownership.

# CHAPTER ONE

## GETTING STARTED WITH SALTWATER AQUARIUMS

Embarking on the journey of setting up a saltwater aquarium can be both exciting and overwhelming, especially for beginners. In this section, we'll break down the key elements to get you started, covering everything from choosing the right tank to understanding saltwater chemistry and essential equipment. Let's dive into the fundamentals of creating a thriving reef tank.

## CHOOSING THE RIGHT AQUARIUM FOR YOUR REEF TANK

The first step in creating your reef tank is selecting the right aquarium. Reef tanks come in various sizes and shapes, each suited to different types of marine life and aesthetic preferences. When choosing your tank, consider the following:

• Glass vs. Acrylic: Glass aquariums are more scratch-resistant and provide better clarity, but they are heavier and more prone to breaking. Acrylic tanks are lighter and offer greater flexibility in shape but can scratch more easily.

• Tank Shape: Standard rectangular tanks are common, but you can also opt for bow-front or corner tanks, which offer unique views and aesthetics.

• Pre-Drilled vs. Standard Tanks: Pre-drilled tanks come with built-in overflow systems, ideal for saltwater setups. Standard tanks can be modified but may require additional equipment for filtration.

## DIFFERENT TYPES OF REEF TANKS

There are several types of reef tanks, each with its own focus and requirements:

• Fish-Only with Live Rock (FOWLR): This type of tank features fish and live rock but minimal or no corals. It's an excellent option for beginners who want to enjoy marine fish without the complexity of coral care.

• Soft Coral Reef Tanks: These tanks are home to soft corals like leather corals, mushrooms, and zoanthids. They are easier to maintain and can thrive with moderate lighting and lower water flow.

• LPS Coral Tanks: Featuring Large Polyp Stony (LPS) corals, these tanks require a bit more expertise and careful management of water parameters.

• SPS Coral Tanks: Small Polyp Stony (SPS) corals are beautiful but delicate and demand more advanced care, including precise water chemistry and intense lighting.

# IDEAL TANK SIZE FOR BEGINNERS

When starting, it's tempting to choose a smaller tank due to space or cost considerations, but a larger tank is often easier to maintain. Here's why:

• Stability: Larger tanks have more water volume, which helps stabilize fluctuations in water parameters like temperature and salinity.

• Easier Maintenance: Larger tanks give you more room to work with when performing maintenance, such as water changes and cleaning.

• Stocking Flexibility: With a bigger tank, you can house a wider variety of fish and corals, giving you more options as your reef tank evolves.

A 30-gallon tank is a good starting point for beginners, but if you have the space, a 55-gallon or larger tank will be even more forgiving.

# PLANNING YOUR SPACE FOR AN AQUARIUM

Before setting up your aquarium, plan where it will go. Consider factors like:

• Size and Location: Ensure the space can accommodate the size of your tank and that it is sturdy enough to support the weight. Also, choose a location that avoids direct sunlight, as it can lead to excessive algae growth.

• Proximity to Electrical Outlets: Make sure the tank is near electrical outlets for equipment like pumps, filters, and lights.

• Accessibility: You'll need easy access to the tank for maintenance tasks like cleaning, water changes, and equipment adjustments.

• Aesthetic Integration: Consider how the tank will fit into your living space. A well-placed tank can become a stunning centerpiece in your home.

# UNDERSTANDING SALTWATER AQUARIUMS

Saltwater aquariums mimic the natural environment of the ocean, and they require a few key elements to thrive. Here's what you need to understand:

• Salinity: The water must have the right salt concentration (typically 1.023–1.025 specific gravity) to support marine life.

• Marine Life Compatibility: Saltwater aquariums host a variety of species, including fish, corals, invertebrates, and live rock. These species rely on a stable environment and compatible tank mates to thrive.

• Water Parameters: Consistently monitoring and adjusting parameters such as pH, temperature, salinity, and nitrates is crucial to the health of your tank.

# THE BASICS OF SALTWATER CHEMISTRY

The success of a saltwater aquarium depends heavily on maintaining the right water chemistry. Here are some critical parameters to monitor:

• pH: Saltwater aquariums should maintain a pH between 7.8 and 8.5. A stable pH is vital for the health of fish and corals.

• Alkalinity: Alkalinity helps stabilize the pH and prevents harmful fluctuations. A target range is 8–12 dKH (degrees of carbonate hardness).

• Calcium: Corals, particularly stony corals, require calcium to grow. Aim for a calcium level of 400–450 ppm.

• Nitrate and Ammonia: These compounds should be kept at low levels to prevent harmful algae blooms and toxicity. Ammonia should be undetectable, while nitrates should stay below 20 ppm.

**Filtration, Lighting, and Water Movement**

Proper filtration, lighting, and water movement are essential to create a healthy reef tank:

• Filtration: A good filtration system will help remove waste, toxins, and debris from the water. Options include protein skimmers, hang-on-back filters, and sump filtration systems.

• Lighting: Reef tanks require lighting that supports coral growth. Different types of lighting include LED, metal halide, and T5 fluorescent. The right light spectrum and intensity depend on the type of corals you plan to keep.

• Water Movement: Corals and fish require a consistent flow of water to thrive. A combination of powerheads and wave makers will ensure adequate water circulation in the tank.

# COMMON MISTAKES TO AVOID

Starting a reef tank can be daunting, and many beginners make a few common mistakes. Here are some to watch out for:

• Overstocking: Adding too many fish or corals too quickly can overwhelm the system and lead to poor water quality.

• Ignoring Water Parameters: Regularly test your water and stay on top of water changes to keep parameters within the ideal range.

• Incompatible Species: Not all fish and corals are compatible. Research the needs and behaviors of potential tank mates to avoid aggression and stress.

• Skipping the Cycle: The nitrogen cycle is essential for establishing a healthy tank. Skipping or rushing through this process can lead to ammonia and nitrite spikes, which are harmful to marine life.

• Neglecting Equipment Maintenance: Regular maintenance of filters, heaters, and other equipment is crucial to prevent malfunctions and maintain optimal tank conditions. By following these foundational guidelines, you'll be well on your way to setting up a beautiful and thriving reef tank. Take your time, plan carefully, and remember that patience is key in the world of saltwater aquariums.

## THE ESSENTIAL EQUIPMENT

Setting up a successful saltwater reef tank involves more than just selecting the right fish and corals—it also requires investing in the right equipment. In this section, we'll explore the essential tools you need to create a thriving aquatic environment, from the tank itself to the crucial systems that maintain water quality, lighting, and overall health. With the right equipment in place, you'll be able to maintain a balanced, healthy reef tank that supports vibrant marine life.

## ESSENTIAL TANK SETUP

Before diving into the specifics of equipment, it's important to start with a proper tank setup. The tank serves as the foundation for your reef, and the right size and configuration will make all the difference.

• Tank: As discussed in Part 1, choosing the right tank size is crucial. A tank that is too small can lead to rapid fluctuations in water parameters, while a larger tank offers more room for fish and corals and provides more stable water conditions. Choose a tank that fits your space, aesthetic preferences, and intended stock.

• Stand: Your tank needs a sturdy stand that can support its weight. Saltwater tanks, especially larger ones, can be very heavy when filled with water, so choose a stand that is both stable and made for aquarium use. Many stands are designed to also house equipment like sumps and filtration systems.

• Sump System: A sump is an additional filtration chamber located beneath the main display tank. It serves multiple purposes, including increasing water volume for better stability, providing extra space for filtration equipment, and helping to hide unsightly components. While optional, a sump system is highly recommended for more advanced reef tanks.

## Protein Skimmers, Heaters, and Other Must-Have Tools

To maintain the health of your reef, several key pieces of equipment are required to keep the water clean, the temperature stable, and your inhabitants comfortable.

• Protein Skimmer: A protein skimmer is essential for removing organic waste from the water before it breaks down into harmful substances like ammonia and nitrate. It works by creating tiny bubbles that attract organic particles, which are then removed from the tank. A protein skimmer helps keep water clear and reduces the likelihood of algae blooms.

• Heaters: Marine life thrives in stable temperatures, so maintaining the proper temperature is critical. Heaters ensure that your tank remains at a consistent temperature, typically between 75°F and 80°F (24°C to 27°C), depending on the species. A reliable heater with a built-in thermostat is crucial to prevent temperature fluctuations.

• Other Must-Have Tools:

Thermometer: Monitoring temperature is important for reef health, so invest in a reliable thermometer to ensure the water stays within the ideal range.

Refractometer: A refractometer is used to measure the salinity of your water. Maintaining proper salinity (typically 1.023–1.025 specific gravity) is vital for the well-being of your marine life.

Water Test Kits: Regularly testing your water for essential parameters (pH, ammonia, nitrites, nitrates, calcium, alkalinity) is crucial for maintaining a balanced reef tank.

Auto Top-Off System: As water evaporates from your tank, it's important to top it off with fresh water to maintain proper salinity levels. An automatic top-off (ATO) system can make this process easier and more consistent.

# CREATING THE PERFECT ENVIRONMENT FOR YOUR REEF

A thriving reef tank is more than just water and equipment—it's about creating a balanced environment that mimics the natural ocean habitat. The right equipment will help you recreate this environment.

• Water Quality: Filtration is key to maintaining high water quality in your reef tank. A combination of mechanical, chemical, and biological filtration is ideal. Use a high-quality protein skimmer to remove dissolved organic waste, a sump system for additional filtration, and live rock for biological filtration.

• Water Circulation: Proper water flow is essential for keeping corals and other tank inhabitants healthy. Invest in a good circulation system, including powerheads and wave makers, to ensure that water moves around the tank evenly, providing your corals with the necessary nutrients and preventing dead spots where waste can accumulate.

• Live Rock: Live rock is not only beautiful but essential for biological filtration. It hosts beneficial bacteria that help break down waste and convert harmful substances into less toxic forms. Live rock also provides hiding spots for fish and helps create a natural-looking environment.

## LIGHTING LED VS METAL HALIDE

Lighting is one of the most important aspects of reef tank care, especially if you plan to keep corals. Proper lighting supports photosynthesis in corals and provides the right intensity and spectrum for their growth.

• LED Lighting: LED lights are the most popular choice for modern reef tanks. They are energy-efficient, produce less heat, and can be easily customized to provide specific light spectrums. LEDs are available in adjustable color temperatures, allowing you to tailor the lighting to your reef's specific needs, such as promoting coral growth or enhancing color.

• Metal Halide Lighting: Metal halide lights are powerful and produce intense light, which is beneficial for SPS (Small Polyp Stony) corals that require high light intensity. However, they are more energy-hungry, produce more heat, and can be more expensive to maintain compared to LEDs. Many advanced hobbyists use metal halide lights for high-light corals, but for most beginners, LEDs are the better choice.

# TEMPERATURE AND WATER FLOW MANAGEMENT

Maintaining stable temperature and water flow are essential for keeping your reef tank healthy and stress-free.

• Temperature Control: Marine fish and corals require stable temperatures to thrive. In addition to your heater, it's important to regularly check the tank temperature and ensure it remains within the ideal range. Avoid large temperature fluctuations, which can stress your reef inhabitants.

• Water Flow: Proper water flow is critical for a reef tank. Different corals have different water flow needs, but most reefs benefit from gentle, consistent movement. Powerheads, wave makers, and adjustable flow pumps can help you achieve the right balance of water movement for your tank's inhabitants.

# CHOOSING THE RIGHT SUBSTRATE FOR YOUR REEF

The substrate in your reef tank plays a crucial role in supporting marine life. It helps anchor corals, provides a home for beneficial bacteria, and can add to the aesthetic of your tank. Here are the common types of substrates for reef tanks:

• Live Sand: Live sand is a popular choice for reef tanks because it contains beneficial bacteria that help break down waste and maintain a healthy environment. It also helps to maintain the proper pH and alkalinity levels in the tank.

• Crushed Coral: Crushed coral is another option for substrate, although it is typically less effective at supporting beneficial bacteria than live sand. It can help maintain higher pH levels but may promote the growth of unwanted algae if not properly maintained.

• Aragonite Sand: Aragonite is a mineral substrate that helps maintain stable calcium and alkalinity levels in the tank. It is ideal for reef tanks because it supports the growth of coral and is a natural material for marine environments. Equipped with the right tank setup, filtration, lighting, and water flow systems, you will be well on your way to creating a successful reef tank. The essential equipment covered in this section is critical for maintaining the delicate balance required to support a thriving reef ecosystem. By investing in quality equipment and ensuring the right setup, you're setting the stage for a beautiful and healthy saltwater aquarium.

# CHAPTER TWO

## MARINE FISH SELECTION AND CARE

When it comes to a saltwater reef tank, selecting the right fish is one of the most rewarding and important aspects of the hobby. Marine fish not only add color and movement to your aquarium but also contribute to the health of the ecosystem. This section will guide you through the process of choosing, caring for, and maintaining your fish, ensuring they thrive in your reef environment.

## CHOOSING FISH FOR YOUR REEF TANK

Choosing fish for your reef tank can be an exciting yet overwhelming task, especially with so many species to choose from. The goal is to create a balanced tank where your fish, corals, and other invertebrates can coexist harmoniously.

• Compatibility: It's important to select fish that are compatible with each other and with the corals you plan to keep. Some fish are aggressive and may prey on smaller species or corals, while others are peaceful and will coexist well with most tankmates.

• Water Requirements: Ensure the fish you choose are suited to the specific water parameters of your reef tank. Different species have varying needs when it comes to temperature, salinity, and pH levels.

• Size and Growth Rate: Take into account the adult size of the fish and whether they will outgrow your tank. Some fish grow quickly and can outgrow smaller tanks, so research the mature size of each species before adding them to your reef.

# BEST BEGINNER FISH FOR REEF TANKS

Starting with the right fish makes the reef-keeping experience much easier and more enjoyable. Some fish are better suited for beginners because they are hardy, adaptable, and relatively easy to care for.

• Clownfish: A classic choice for beginners, clownfish are hardy and adapt well to most reef environments. They're also known for their symbiotic relationship with sea anemones, although they can live without them in the tank.

• Damselfish: Damselfish are small, colorful, and active. While some species can be territorial, many are peaceful and easy to care for, making them an excellent choice for beginners.

• Royal Gramma: This small, vibrant fish is not only beautiful but also hardy and easy to care for.

Royal Grammas are typically peaceful and get along with most other tankmates.

• Green Chromis: Known for their peaceful nature and schooling behavior, Green Chromis are excellent additions to a reef tank. They add a shimmering blue-green color and are great for beginners.

• Blennies and Gobies: These bottom-dwelling fish are great for reef tanks because they help stir the sand and eat algae. They are peaceful, hardy, and easy to care for, making them ideal for novice reef keepers.

## REEF SAFE VS NON-REEF SAFE FISH

When selecting fish, one of the most critical factors to consider is whether they are "reef safe." Reef-safe fish will not harm or eat your corals, while non-reef-safe fish may pose a threat to the delicate ecosystem of your tank.

• Reef Safe Fish: These fish are generally peaceful and will not harm corals or invertebrates. Popular reef-safe fish include clownfish, tangs, wrasses, gobies, and chromis. These fish are great for maintaining the balance of your reef tank.

• Non-Reef Safe Fish: Some fish are known to eat or damage corals, snails, or other invertebrates. For example, certain angelfish, triggerfish, and pufferfish may nibble on corals or other creatures. If you have delicate corals or invertebrates in your tank, it's best to avoid these species.

## UNDERSTANDING FISH COMPATIBILITY

Fish compatibility is essential to maintaining a peaceful and healthy reef tank. Some fish are territorial or aggressive, while others are peaceful and will get along with a wide range of tankmates. When selecting fish, consider their behavior and ensure that the species you choose can live together without conflict.

• Aggressive Fish: Some fish species, like the larger groupers or certain types of triggerfish, can be aggressive towards other fish, especially if they are of a similar size or have similar colors. They may bully or attack other species, leading to stress and injury.

• Peaceful Fish: Most reef-safe species, such as clownfish, wrasses, and gobies, are peaceful and get along well with others. These fish help create a balanced and harmonious tank environment.

• Schooling Fish: Fish that prefer to school, like chromis or anthias, are ideal for a reef tank because they stay together in groups and are usually less aggressive towards other species.

# FISH CARE

Proper fish care is vital for keeping your marine life healthy and happy in a reef tank. Fish require consistent monitoring, attention to their needs, and good practices for feeding and health.

• Water Quality: Fish thrive in clean, stable water conditions. Regular water changes, proper filtration, and monitoring key water parameters (such as ammonia, nitrite, nitrate, salinity, and pH) are crucial for maintaining a healthy environment for your fish.

• Feeding: Feed your fish a varied diet that includes both dry and frozen foods, such as flakes, pellets, and frozen mysis shrimp or brine shrimp. Be sure to avoid overfeeding, as excess food can pollute the water and lead to algae blooms.

• Behavior Observation: Regularly observe your fish for signs of stress, illness, or aggression. Healthy fish should be active, have clear eyes, and show normal feeding behavior. Any changes in behavior, such as hiding, lethargy, or abnormal swimming, may indicate a health issue.

## FEEDING, HEALTH, AND DISEASE PREVENTION

Feeding and health care are essential components of keeping your marine fish healthy.

• Feeding: Offer a balanced diet to meet the nutritional needs of your fish. Herbivores like tangs and rabbitfish should be provided with algae-based foods, while carnivores like lionfish and groupers require protein-rich foods.

• Disease Prevention: Regular water quality checks, quarantine procedures, and stress reduction are key to preventing disease. Keeping new fish in quarantine for a couple of weeks before introducing them to the main tank is a good practice to avoid introducing potential pathogens.

• Common Diseases: Fish in reef tanks can be susceptible to diseases like ich (white spot disease), marine velvet, and fungal infections. Early detection and treatment are important, and medicated food or freshwater dips can be used to treat some common ailments.

## ACCLIMATING FISH TO YOUR REEF TANK

Acclimating new fish to your reef tank is a delicate process that helps prevent shock and stress. Here are the steps to follow when introducing new fish:

• Drip Acclimation: This method involves slowly adding small amounts of tank water to the bag or container holding your new fish. Over the course of 30-60 minutes, gradually acclimate the fish to the temperature and water parameters of your tank.

• Float the Bag: Start by floating the bag with the fish in your tank for about 15-20 minutes to equalize the temperature. Then, begin the drip acclimation process.

• Release the Fish: Once acclimated, gently release the fish into the tank, avoiding sudden movements that could startle or stress the fish.

## MAINTAINING FISH HEALTH LONG-TERM

Long-term fish health requires consistent care and maintenance of both the fish and their environment. Here's how to ensure the continued well-being of your marine fish:

• Regular Water Changes: Weekly or bi-weekly water changes are essential to keeping the tank water clean and removing waste products. This helps maintain a stable environment for your fish and reduces the likelihood of disease.

• Monitor Fish Behavior: Keep an eye on your fish for any changes in behavior or appearance.

Healthy fish are usually active, feed well, and swim confidently. Any signs of stress or illness should be addressed immediately.

• Provide Hiding Places: Many fish, especially those that are more shy or stressed, benefit from having places to hide. Live rock, caves, and aquarium decorations provide shelter and help reduce stress.

Selecting and caring for marine fish is one of the most rewarding parts of maintaining a reef tank. By carefully choosing compatible fish, providing proper care, and maintaining a healthy tank environment, you can enjoy the beauty and diversity that marine fish bring to your aquarium. With proper attention to feeding, health, and disease prevention, your fish will thrive in the stunning ecosystem you've worked hard to create.

# CORALS AND INVERTEBRATES

Corals and invertebrates are the foundation of a vibrant and diverse reef tank. Not only do they add breathtaking color and texture, but they also contribute to the biological filtration of your tank. This section will guide you through understanding coral care, choosing the right types of corals, and managing the invertebrates that help maintain a balanced reef ecosystem.

## THE BASICS OF CORAL CARE

Corals are living organisms that rely on stable water conditions to thrive. Their care requires a good understanding of their environmental needs and the right equipment to maintain those conditions. Here are the essential aspects of coral care:

• Lighting: Corals require high-intensity lighting to perform photosynthesis. The right lighting helps corals grow and maintain vibrant colors. Different types of corals have varying lighting needs, but in general, reef tanks should have powerful lighting, such as LED or metal halide lamps, to mimic the natural sunlight they would receive in the ocean.

• Water Parameters: Corals need stable water conditions. Key parameters like temperature, salinity, pH, and calcium levels must be carefully maintained. Regular testing of the water is essential for ensuring a healthy environment for your corals.

• Flow: Proper water movement is necessary to ensure that corals receive nutrients and oxygen while also removing waste. The flow in a reef tank should be gentle but consistent, providing the right conditions for coral health.

# TYPES OF CORALS SOFT VS HARD CORALS

Corals can be classified into two main categories: soft corals and hard corals. Each has different care requirements and behaviors, so it's important to understand their differences when choosing which types to add to your tank.

• Soft Corals: These corals are typically more flexible and easier to care for, making them ideal for beginners. Soft corals, such as leathers, mushrooms, and zoanthids, are less demanding in terms of water conditions and lighting. They don't produce calcium skeletons like hard corals and instead have a soft, fleshy body that sways with the water flow.

• Hard Corals: Also known as stony corals, these corals have a calcium carbonate skeleton that helps to build the reef structure. Hard corals, including brain, acropora, and montipora, require more stable water conditions, high light intensity, and stronger water flow. They are more sensitive to changes in water quality but are key to building the backbone of a reef tank due to their ability to create a calcium skeleton.

## HOW TO CHOOSE THE RIGHT CORALS FOR YOUR REEF

Choosing the right corals for your reef tank depends on various factors, including the tank's lighting, water parameters, and the fish and invertebrates already in place. Here's what to consider when selecting corals:

• Compatibility with Tankmates: Some fish and invertebrates, such as certain types of snails or herbivorous fish, may damage or feed on corals. Be sure to research which fish are reef-safe before adding them to your tank.

• Lighting Requirements: Different corals have different lighting needs. Some soft corals can thrive under lower light conditions, while most hard corals require intense lighting to thrive. Make sure the corals you choose match the intensity and spectrum of light your tank can provide.

• Tank Size and Flow: Larger tanks can support a wider variety of corals due to more stable water parameters and better space for growth. Also, consider the flow rate in your tank, as some corals need a gentle flow while others thrive with strong currents.

## CORAL PLACEMENT AND GROWTH

Placement and growth are critical for coral care, as each species has specific space and environmental needs.

• Space and Positioning: Corals need sufficient space to grow without overcrowding each other. Avoid placing fast-growing corals near slow growers to ensure they aren't shaded out or smothered.

• Top vs. Bottom Placement: Generally, hard corals prefer to be placed higher in the tank, where they can get more light, while soft corals can be placed lower down in less intense light. However, it depends on the species, so always research the specific light and flow needs of the corals you choose.

• Growth Rate: Some corals grow quickly and may require more frequent pruning to avoid overcrowding, while others grow slowly and can be left to thrive over time. Monitoring their growth and health regularly is important to ensure they don't outgrow their space.

# CHAPTER THREE

## UNDERSTANDING INVERTEBRATES IN REEF TANKS

Invertebrates play vital roles in a reef tank, from maintaining water quality to adding beauty and diversity. These creatures help balance the ecosystem by consuming algae, detritus, and other organic material. Key types of invertebrates include:

• Crustaceans: Crabs, shrimp, and lobsters are important members of the reef ecosystem. They help clean the tank by eating algae, uneaten food, and detritus. Some species, like cleaner shrimp, also form symbiotic relationships with fish, cleaning parasites from their bodies.

• Snails: Snails, including turbo snails and trochus snails, help with algae control by grazing on the surfaces of rocks, corals, and the tank glass. Snails also help aerate the substrate, promoting a healthy environment for all tank inhabitants.

## CRABS, SHRIMP, AND SNAILS ROLES IN YOUR TANK

• Crabs: Crabs, such as hermit crabs, are excellent scavengers that help clean up uneaten food and detritus. Some species may also help aerate the substrate by digging and moving sand. However, be cautious when choosing crabs, as some species may become aggressive or compete with snails for shells.

• Shrimp: Shrimp, like cleaner shrimp and peppermint shrimp, are beneficial for maintaining a healthy reef tank. Cleaner shrimp will remove parasites from the fish, and peppermint shrimp are known for their ability to eat certain pests, like aiptasia anemones.

• Snails: Snails serve as natural algae eaters, keeping your tank's surfaces clean. Some snails, such as nassarius snails, also help clean up detritus by burrowing into the substrate. Adding a variety of snails can be a great way to manage algae growth and keep your tank clean.

## MAINTAINING A BALANCED REEF ECOSYSTEM

Creating and maintaining a balanced reef ecosystem involves more than just adding fish and corals. The interaction between corals, invertebrates, and other tank inhabitants must be carefully managed to maintain stability.

• Water Quality: Invertebrates and corals are particularly sensitive to changes in water quality. Ensure your water parameters remain stable, and perform regular water changes to keep the tank environment healthy for all inhabitants.

• Nutrient Levels: Keep an eye on nutrient levels such as nitrates and phosphates. High nutrient levels can lead to algae blooms that can smother corals and invertebrates. A good protein skimmer, regular water changes, and careful feeding practices help keep nutrients in check.

• Diversified Cleanup Crew: A diverse cleanup crew consisting of various snails, crabs, and shrimp helps maintain a balanced reef by keeping algae under control, scavenging uneaten food, and providing essential ecosystem services.

Corals and invertebrates are essential to the health and beauty of your reef tank. With proper care, a variety of soft and hard corals can thrive and grow, while invertebrates play vital roles in cleaning and maintaining the ecosystem. By understanding the needs of each species and maintaining stable water conditions, you can create a stunning, balanced reef that will provide years of enjoyment and fascination.

# WATER QUALITY AND MAINTENANCE

Maintaining optimal water quality is crucial for the success of your reef tank. It affects the health of your fish, corals, and invertebrates, and ensures that your tank remains stable and vibrant. In this section, we'll cover the essential water parameters you need to monitor, as well as the best practices for maintaining a clean and healthy environment for your reef.

## MONITORING AND TESTING WATER PARAMETERS

Regular testing and monitoring of water parameters are key to keeping your reef tank healthy. You'll need to test for several critical parameters to ensure that your tank's water remains within the ideal range for your marine life.

• Test Kits and Meters: Invest in reliable test kits or digital meters for key parameters like pH, ammonia, nitrites, nitrates, and calcium. Test kits are available in both liquid and strip formats, while digital meters offer more precision.

• Consistency: It's important to test the water regularly, at least once a week, to catch any fluctuations early. Keeping a water testing log can help you track trends and detect potential issues before they become problems.

## UNDERSTANDING PH, AMMONIA, NITRITES, AND NITRATES

Each of these water parameters plays a crucial role in maintaining a healthy environment for your reef tank inhabitants.

• pH: The pH level of your reef tank water indicates its acidity or alkalinity. The ideal pH for a reef tank is between 8.0 and 8.4. If the pH drops too low or rises too high, it can stress out your corals and fish. Regular water changes and proper calcium dosing can help maintain stable pH levels.

• Ammonia: Ammonia is toxic to marine life, and even small amounts can be harmful to your fish and corals. Ammonia levels should always be at 0 ppm (parts per million) in a healthy reef tank. Elevated ammonia levels usually indicate poor filtration or an overstocked tank.

• Nitrites: Nitrites are also toxic and should be kept at 0 ppm. Nitrites are typically present during the initial stages of setting up a reef tank, as part of the nitrogen cycle. They are usually converted into nitrates by beneficial bacteria in the tank's filtration system.

• Nitrates: Nitrates are the final byproduct of the nitrogen cycle and are less harmful than ammonia or nitrites, but high levels (above 20-30 ppm) can still cause problems, such as promoting unwanted algae growth. Regular water changes, protein skimming, and having live rock and a good clean-up crew help keep nitrate levels under control.

## SALINITY AND ITS IMPORTANCE IN A REEF TANK

Salinity refers to the concentration of dissolved salts in the water and is one of the most important parameters for marine tanks. For reef tanks, the ideal salinity is typically between 1.023 and 1.025 specific gravity (SG).

• Hydrometer and Refractometer: Use a hydrometer or, preferably, a refractometer to measure salinity accurately. The refractometer is more precise and less prone to errors, making it the preferred choice for reef keepers.

• Stability: Maintaining stable salinity is crucial for the health of your reef tank inhabitants. Sudden changes in salinity can lead to stress, illness, or even death in sensitive species like corals. Always check salinity when performing water changes or adding new saltwater.

• Adjustment: If your salinity levels are off, you can adjust them by adding more salt or freshwater, but make changes gradually to avoid stressing the tank's inhabitants.

## REGULAR MAINTENANCE ROUTINES

Regular maintenance is essential for ensuring the long-term success of your reef tank. The routine tasks include water testing, water changes, and cleaning the tank and equipment. Keeping a consistent maintenance schedule will help you stay on top of your tank's health and prevent major issues from arising.

• Daily: Check the water temperature, lighting, and equipment such as pumps and filters. Ensure that all equipment is running smoothly.

• Weekly: Test water parameters (pH, ammonia, nitrites, nitrates, salinity) and make any necessary adjustments. Inspect fish and corals for signs of disease or stress. Clean the tank glass and remove any debris from the substrate.

• Biweekly or Monthly: Perform a partial water change, typically about 10-15% of the tank's total volume. This helps to maintain water quality, replenish essential trace elements, and remove excess nutrients. Clean and inspect filters, protein skimmers, and heaters.

## WEEKLY, MONTHLY, AND QUARTERLY MAINTENANCE TASKS

Keeping track of more detailed maintenance tasks will ensure the longevity and health of your reef tank.

Weekly Tasks

• Test Water Parameters: Check for pH, ammonia, nitrites, nitrates, and salinity.

• Clean the Glass: Use a scraper or magnet cleaner to remove algae from the glass.

• Remove Detritus: Use a siphon to remove uneaten food, detritus, and waste from the substrate.

• Inspect Equipment: Check the functionality of pumps, protein skimmers, and other equipment. Clean them if necessary.

Monthly Tasks

• Partial Water Change: Replace about 10-15% of the tank's water with fresh saltwater.

• Clean the Filter: Rinse out the filter media with tank water to remove accumulated debris.

• Trim Corals: If necessary, trim fast-growing corals to maintain proper tank balance and prevent overcrowding.

Quarterly Tasks

• Deep Cleaning: Clean the tank's decorations, rocks, and equipment, including the protein skimmer and sump. Perform a thorough check for any salt creep buildup and remove it.

• Test for Trace Elements: Test for trace elements like calcium, magnesium, and alkalinity. If necessary, add supplements to maintain ideal levels.

• Inspect Livestock: Check on the health of your fish, corals, and invertebrates. Remove any deceased or stressed-out organisms and adjust your tank parameters accordingly.

# CLEANING YOUR TANK, EQUIPMENT, AND DECORATIONS

Keeping your tank and equipment clean is essential for a healthy reef tank. Regular cleaning prevents the buildup of organic matter, reduces algae growth, and ensures that your filtration and circulation systems are functioning optimally.

• Tank Cleaning: Wipe down the interior glass to remove algae buildup. Use a magnet cleaner for easier cleaning of the tank's walls. If your tank has a sump or filtration compartment, clean those areas regularly to prevent clogging.

• Equipment Maintenance: Clean your protein skimmer, filter, and pumps regularly to ensure efficient operation. Follow the manufacturer's instructions for maintenance, and inspect each piece of equipment for signs of wear and tear.

• Decorations and Rocks: While you don't want to disrupt your reef too much, cleaning decorations and live rock can help prevent algae buildup. Use a toothbrush or soft brush to gently scrub off any unwanted growths.

Maintaining good water quality is the backbone of a thriving reef tank. By consistently monitoring and adjusting key water parameters such as pH, ammonia, nitrites, nitrates, and salinity, you'll create an environment where your fish, corals, and invertebrates can thrive. Regular maintenance routines—weekly, monthly, and quarterly—help keep your tank clean, your equipment working efficiently, and your livestock healthy. With attention to detail and dedication, your reef tank can remain a beautiful, sustainable ecosystem for years to come.

# REEF TANK TROUBLESHOOTING

Even the most carefully maintained reef tanks can encounter problems from time to time. Whether it's an unexpected spike in algae growth, signs of illness in your fish or corals, or water quality issues, knowing how to troubleshoot effectively will ensure that your tank remains healthy and thriving. In this section, we'll explore common reef tank problems and how to handle them.

## COMMON PROBLEMS IN SALTWATER AQUARIUMS

Reef tanks are complex ecosystems, and issues can arise unexpectedly. Recognizing common problems early is the key to keeping your tank in balance.

• Algae Growth: Algae blooms are one of the most common issues in reef tanks. These blooms can be caused by excess nutrients (such as nitrates and phosphates), poor water quality, or too much light. While some algae growth is normal and part of the tank's natural balance, excessive algae can smother corals, clog equipment, and make the tank look unappealing.

• Fish Diseases: Fish are susceptible to a variety of diseases, ranging from minor skin issues to more serious illnesses like ich (white spot disease), velvet, and fin rot. Stress, poor water quality, and incompatible tank mates can weaken fish and make them more vulnerable to diseases.

• Coral Stress: Corals can become stressed from fluctuating water conditions, poor lighting, or being placed in a tank with incompatible fish. Signs of stressed corals include bleaching (when they lose their color) or closing up for extended periods.

• Poor Water Quality: Imbalances in the water's chemical composition, such as high ammonia or low alkalinity, can quickly deteriorate the health of your reef tank inhabitants. It's important to regularly test the water and address any discrepancies.

## ALGAE BLOOM AND HOW TO CONTROL IT

Algae blooms are often the result of excess nutrients like nitrates and phosphates in the water. They can be unsightly and harmful to your reef tank's ecosystem, suffocating corals and clogging filtration systems.

• Causes of Algae Bloom: Common causes include overfeeding, poor filtration, too much light, or decaying organic matter.

• Preventing Algae Growth: To prevent algae blooms, maintain a strict feeding regimen to avoid excess nutrients, perform regular water changes, and ensure that your filtration system is working effectively.

• Controlling Algae:

Reduce Lighting: Cut back on light cycles to reduce algae growth. A light cycle of 8-10 hours a day is ideal for most reef tanks.

Increase Water Movement: Strong water flow can help prevent algae from settling on surfaces.

Introduce Algae-Eating Invertebrates: Snails, crabs, and certain fish species like tangs are natural algae eaters and can help control algae growth.

Use Phosphate Removers: Using a phosphate-removing media in your filter can help lower phosphates in the tank, reducing the nutrients that algae need to thrive.

## DEALING WITH DISEASE IN FISH AND CORALS

Fish and corals are vulnerable to diseases, many of which can spread quickly in a closed aquarium environment. Monitoring your reef tank's inhabitants and recognizing symptoms of illness early are key to preventing and managing disease outbreaks.

• Fish Disease Prevention:

Quarantine New Fish: Always quarantine new fish for at least two weeks before introducing them into your main tank to avoid introducing parasites or diseases.

Signs of Illness: Common signs of disease in fish include scratching against objects, lesions, abnormal swimming, loss of appetite, and faded colors.

Treatment: If your fish show signs of illness, move them to a quarantine tank and treat them with medications designed for the specific disease. Always follow the instructions carefully, as some treatments can harm corals or invertebrates.

• Coral Disease and Stress:

Signs of Coral Stress: Corals that are not opening, have faded or discolored tissue, or have brown spots or film on them may be stressed. Corals are particularly sensitive to changes in water quality.

Addressing Coral Illness: Test and correct water parameters. If necessary, move the coral to a different location in the tank with better lighting or water flow. If the coral is severely stressed, removing it to a quarantine tank for treatment can sometimes help.

Fragging: If a coral is infected or dying, you may be able to save healthy parts of it by cutting off the affected sections (fragging) and allowing them to regrow in better conditions.

# FIXING WATER QUALITY ISSUES

Water quality is critical for the health of your reef tank. Poor water quality can lead to a host of problems, including algae blooms, stress in your fish and corals, and disease outbreaks. Common water quality issues include incorrect pH, ammonia spikes, high nitrate levels, and low oxygen.

• Check and Adjust pH: If your pH is too low (acidic) or too high (alkaline), it can stress your marine life. Use a pH buffer to raise or lower the pH to the ideal range (typically between 8.0 and 8.4 for reef tanks).

• Ammonia and Nitrite Spikes: Elevated ammonia or nitrites are signs of poor filtration or an imbalance in the nitrogen cycle. Perform a water change immediately, increase the biological filtration, and check your protein skimmer and filter media for cleaning.

• High Nitrate Levels: If nitrates exceed 20-30 ppm, consider reducing feeding, adding nitrate-absorbing media, or increasing water changes. Excessive nitrates can lead to poor coral health and promote algae growth.

## IDENTIFYING AND CORRECTING WATER IMBALANCES

In addition to pH, ammonia, nitrites, and nitrates, there are other water imbalances that can affect the health of your reef tank, such as low calcium, magnesium, or alkalinity.

• Calcium and Alkalinity: Corals rely on calcium and alkalinity to build their skeletons. Test and maintain appropriate levels of both. Calcium should generally be between 400 and 450 ppm, and alkalinity should be between 8-12 dKH.

• Magnesium: Magnesium helps maintain calcium and alkalinity balance in the tank. Test magnesium regularly, aiming for levels between 1250 and 1350 ppm.

• Supplementation: If any of these elements are low, use appropriate supplements to bring the levels back to normal. Make adjustments gradually to avoid shocking your system.

## MANAGING NITROGEN CYCLES AND BIOLOGICAL FILTRATION

The nitrogen cycle is crucial for establishing a balanced and healthy reef tank. Beneficial bacteria break down harmful compounds like ammonia and nitrites, converting them into nitrates, which are less toxic.

• Cycle Establishment: When setting up a new reef tank, allow the nitrogen cycle to establish itself before adding fish or corals. This can take several weeks, during which ammonia and nitrites will spike before stabilizing.

• Biological Filtration: Your tank's biological filter (live rock, sand, and biological filter media) is key to maintaining the nitrogen cycle. Ensure your tank has enough surface area for beneficial bacteria to thrive. If necessary, add additional live rock or filter media to increase filtration capacity.

Troubleshooting your reef tank involves a combination of vigilance, understanding, and timely intervention. Common problems like algae blooms, fish diseases, water quality issues, and coral stress can be managed by identifying the signs early, correcting water imbalances, and ensuring your tank's ecosystem remains stable. Regular monitoring, proper maintenance, and an understanding of how the nitrogen cycle and biological filtration work will help you keep your reef tank thriving for years to come.

# CHAPTER FOUR

# ADVANCED REEF TANK TECHNIQUES

As you gain experience and confidence in managing a reef tank, you'll likely want to take your hobby to the next level. Advanced reef tank techniques involve understanding complex coral and fish care, utilizing automation for maintenance, and experimenting with propagation. This section will guide you through the process of upgrading your reef tank, adding more challenging species, and adopting new techniques that will allow you to elevate your aquarium to a thriving, advanced ecosystem.

# UPGRADING YOUR REEF TANK FOR ADVANCED HOBBYISTS

Once you've mastered the basics of reef tank care, upgrading your setup can open up new possibilities and allow for greater creativity in your tank design. Here are a few steps to consider when planning an upgrade:

• Tank Size and Shape: Larger tanks offer more space for both fish and corals and provide a more stable environment, which can be crucial for maintaining healthy water parameters. Consider moving to a larger tank if you want to add more species or if you're interested in creating a more elaborate aquascape. Tanks with unique shapes, such as corner or peninsula tanks, can also provide more visual interest and flexibility for aquascaping.

• Upgrading Filtration: With larger tanks or more complex setups, you'll need more powerful filtration systems to maintain water quality. Consider upgrading your protein skimmer, adding additional mechanical or biological filtration, and installing a refugium to house beneficial algae and copepods.

• Lighting Upgrades: If you plan on keeping more demanding corals, such as SPS (small polyp stony) corals, you'll need a more powerful lighting system. LED systems with adjustable spectrums or metal halide lights can provide the intense light needed for photosynthetic corals. Be sure to match the lighting to the specific needs of the corals and fish you wish to keep.

• Water Flow: For advanced reef tanks, especially those housing SPS corals, water flow becomes even more critical. Consider adding additional powerheads or wave makers to create strong, variable water currents that mimic the conditions found in the ocean.

## ADDING MORE COMPLEX CORALS AND FISH

As you move into more advanced reef keeping, you'll likely want to introduce a wider variety of corals and fish into your tank. These species often require specific care and more attention to detail.

• Complex Corals: Advanced hobbyists may choose to keep a variety of corals that require more precise conditions to thrive. SPS corals, LPS (large polyp stony) corals, and even delicate species like sun corals or gorgonians fall into this category. These corals often require stronger lighting, higher water flow, and careful monitoring of calcium, alkalinity, and magnesium levels.

• Challenging Fish: Some fish species, such as certain tangs, angelfish, or wrasses, require larger tanks, specific water conditions, and a carefully curated selection of tank mates. Before adding these fish, make sure your tank is fully established and that you can provide the proper care.

• Compatibility: As you introduce more complex species, it becomes even more important to pay attention to compatibility. Some corals and fish species may have aggressive tendencies or specific territorial behaviors. Proper research and planning will help ensure that your new additions coexist peacefully with existing inhabitants.

# THE IMPORTANCE OF ACCLIMATION AND QUARANTINE

Acclimating new additions to your reef tank is essential to minimize stress and prevent the introduction of diseases. Quarantine and acclimation procedures help to ensure that new fish, corals, and invertebrates adapt to your tank's conditions in a safe and controlled manner.

• Acclimation: When introducing new fish or corals to your tank, it's vital to acclimate them slowly to avoid shock. For fish, drip acclimation is a common method that involves slowly mixing water from the tank with the water the fish came in. This allows them to adjust to differences in temperature, salinity, and pH. For corals, gentle placement in lower light or water flow areas can help them adjust before being moved to their final spots.

• Quarantine: Always quarantine new fish, corals, and invertebrates for at least two weeks before introducing them to your main tank. This prevents the spread of diseases like ich, velvet, and other parasitic infections. During quarantine, monitor the new arrivals for signs of illness, and treat them if necessary.

• Preventing Disease: Quarantining and acclimating new additions helps reduce the risk of introducing pests, parasites, and diseases into your reef tank, ensuring a healthier, more stable environment for all inhabitants.

# PROPAGATING CORALS TIPS FOR BEGINNERS

Coral propagation is a rewarding and sustainable way to expand your reef tank. It involves fragging (clipping) a healthy coral and allowing it to grow into a new colony. Here's how you can start propagating corals:

• Selecting Healthy Corals for Fragging: Choose a coral that is thriving and free from disease or stress. SPS corals, like Acropora, and LPS corals, like Euphyllia, are popular choices for propagation.

• Cutting and Fragging: Use specialized coral-cutting tools, such as bone cutters or frag saws, to carefully cut a piece of the coral. Ensure the cut is clean and smooth to avoid damaging the coral. Always frag corals under water to avoid air exposure.

• Mounting the Frag: After cutting the coral, mount the frag onto a piece of live rock, frag plug, or other suitable surface. Secure the frag with coral glue or putty, and place it in a low-light area of your tank to allow it time to heal.

• Feeding and Care: Newly fragged corals may need extra care to ensure they grow successfully. Provide them with appropriate water flow, lighting, and feeding as they adjust and start to grow.

## USING AUTOMATION FOR REEF TANK MAINTENANCE

Automation can greatly simplify reef tank maintenance, making it easier to keep your tank in peak condition with minimal effort.

• Automatic Water Changes: Automated water change systems can monitor the water level and perform scheduled water changes, helping to maintain stable water parameters. This is especially helpful for large tanks where manual water changes can be time-consuming.

• Dosing Pumps: For maintaining proper calcium, alkalinity, and magnesium levels, automated dosing pumps can be used to add supplements to your tank on a scheduled basis. This ensures that levels stay consistent without the need for manual intervention.

• Auto-Top Off (ATO) Systems: Evaporation is inevitable in a reef tank, and an ATO system automatically replenishes evaporated water to maintain the proper salinity and water level. This can be a huge time-saver, ensuring that your tank is always at the right level.

• Lighting and Flow Controllers: Use timers and controllers to automate lighting cycles and water flow patterns, simulating natural day/night cycles and ocean currents. Many modern controllers allow you to set different lighting and flow schedules based on the needs of your tank's inhabitants.

• Monitoring Systems: Advanced reef monitoring systems track key parameters like temperature, pH, salinity, and oxygen levels. These systems provide real-time data and alert you if any parameters fall outside of the safe range, allowing you to address issues quickly.

Advanced reef tank techniques are designed to enhance your reef-keeping experience and take your aquarium to the next level. Upgrading your tank, adding more complex species, and embracing automation and coral propagation can lead to a thriving, dynamic reef ecosystem that's both beautiful and sustainable. Whether you're interested in the delicate art of coral propagation or utilizing cutting-edge technology to maintain your tank, these advanced techniques will allow you to explore the full potential of the reef tank hobby. With dedication, research, and attention to detail, you can create a stunning reef aquarium that's both rewarding to maintain and awe-inspiring to behold.

# THE FUTURE OF SALTWATER AQUARIUMS

The world of saltwater aquariums is constantly evolving, driven by technological advancements, new discoveries in marine science, and a growing commitment to sustainability. As hobbyists and professionals alike strive to create the best possible environments for their fish, corals, and other marine life, the future of reef keeping holds exciting possibilities. In this section, we'll explore some of the innovations shaping the future of saltwater aquariums, how sustainability is becoming a key focus, and how you can continue to grow and learn in this ever-changing hobby.

# INNOVATIVE TECHNOLOGY IN REEF TANKS

Technology plays a pivotal role in the advancement of saltwater aquariums, allowing hobbyists to better manage their tanks and create healthier, more stable ecosystems. Some of the most exciting innovations in reef tank technology include:

• Smart Monitoring Systems: The future of reef keeping is going digital with smart monitoring systems. These systems allow you to track a wide range of parameters like temperature, pH, salinity, nitrates, and calcium levels in real time, all through an app on your smartphone. With these systems, you can receive alerts if any parameters fall out of range, making it easier to address issues before they become serious.

• AI-Powered Automation: Artificial intelligence is beginning to make its mark in reef tank maintenance. Automated systems now use AI to adjust parameters like lighting and water flow based on the behavior of the fish and the needs of your corals. This takes the guesswork out of maintaining optimal tank conditions and helps create a more dynamic and responsive environment.

• LED Lighting Advancements: LED lighting has already revolutionized the reef tank hobby, but future advancements promise even more energy-efficient and customizable options. New LED fixtures are capable of mimicking natural sunlight with greater precision, providing a full spectrum of light that's specifically tuned to support coral growth and health.

• Robotic Cleaners: Robotic tank cleaners, designed to help with cleaning algae and detritus, are becoming increasingly popular. These devices can autonomously roam your tank, removing debris and helping to maintain a cleaner, healthier environment without human intervention.

• Next-Generation Protein Skimmers: Protein skimmers, which remove organic waste from the water, are becoming more efficient and quieter. Some of the new models include features like auto-cleaning, allowing them to maintain optimal performance with less frequent maintenance.

## SUSTAINABILITY AND ECO-FRIENDLY REEF KEEPING

Sustainability is an issue of growing importance in the reef keeping community. With the environmental impact of the aquarium trade on natural reefs becoming more apparent, hobbyists are increasingly looking for ways to reduce their ecological footprint and contribute to the preservation of marine ecosystems. Here are some key trends in sustainable reef keeping:

• Aquaculture and Coral Farming: The practice of farming corals and marine fish in captivity is on the rise. This method reduces the demand for wild-caught species, which can harm natural reefs. Coral farming not only helps protect delicate ecosystems but also allows hobbyists to source their tank inhabitants responsibly. Many coral farms now offer a variety of coral species that are grown specifically for the aquarium trade, ensuring that they are healthy, disease-free, and sustainably harvested.

• Reef-Friendly Products: Many aquarium products are now being made with sustainability in mind. For example, environmentally friendly aquarium substrates, filtration materials, and additives that reduce the impact on natural environments are becoming more widely available. Look for products that are labeled as reef-safe and eco-friendly to minimize your environmental impact.

• Water Conservation: Efficient water usage is another important aspect of sustainable reef keeping. Automated water changes, water filtration systems, and water recycling methods are becoming more common in advanced reef setups. Some systems are designed to minimize water waste while still maintaining optimal conditions for the inhabitants of the tank.

• Energy Efficiency: The energy requirements of a reef tank can be significant, especially when it comes to lighting and filtration systems. The future of reef keeping will likely see even more energy-efficient technologies. LED lighting, low-energy protein skimmers, and energy-saving pumps will continue to reduce the carbon footprint of saltwater aquariums.

• Invasive Species Prevention: Hobbyists are increasingly aware of the potential harm caused by introducing invasive species into the environment. Many reef keepers are now focused on educating themselves about the risks of introducing non-native species into the wild and are working to avoid releasing tank species into natural bodies of water.

## HOW TO CONTINUE LEARNING AND GROWING AS A REEF KEEPER

As the world of reef keeping continues to evolve, staying up-to-date with the latest developments and best practices is crucial for every hobbyist. Fortunately, there are countless resources available to help you grow as a reef keeper. Here's how you can continue learning and advancing your skills:

• Online Communities and Forums: The reef keeping community is active online, with forums, social media groups, and specialized websites offering advice, inspiration, and the latest news. Joining these communities allows you to share experiences, troubleshoot problems, and learn from others who have been in the hobby for years. Sites like Reef2Reef and the Reef Central forum are great places to start.

• Courses and Workshops: Many aquarium shops, clubs, and organizations offer educational courses and workshops on various aspects of reef keeping. Whether you want to learn about coral propagation, advanced water chemistry, or the latest reef tank technology, these resources can provide in-depth learning opportunities from experts in the field.

• Conventions and Trade Shows: Attending reef tank conventions and trade shows is a fantastic way to immerse yourself in the world of saltwater aquariums. These events feature the latest innovations in aquarium technology, provide opportunities to network with other hobbyists, and give you the chance to learn from industry leaders.

• Marine Conservation Efforts: Supporting and participating in marine conservation efforts can further enhance your understanding of the ecosystems you're replicating in your reef tank. By getting involved with organizations like the Coral Triangle Initiative or the Marine Conservation Society, you'll not only be contributing to the preservation of the oceans, but also deepening your knowledge of the delicate balance that supports marine life.

The future of saltwater aquariums is bright, with continued technological advancements, a growing focus on sustainability, and a deepening commitment to marine conservation. By embracing innovative tools and techniques, adopting eco-friendly practices, and remaining curious and engaged with the community, you can be part of this exciting evolution in reef tank keeping. With ongoing learning and a focus on preserving the beauty of the ocean, the future of your saltwater aquarium hobby holds endless possibilities.

# RECAP OF KEY CONCEPTS

Throughout this guide, we've covered essential aspects of saltwater aquariums, starting with the basics of tank setup and progressing to advanced techniques for managing a thriving reef ecosystem. Here are some key takeaways:

• Choosing the Right Tank: The foundation of your reef tank starts with selecting the right aquarium, equipment, and fish. Proper planning ensures a stable environment where both corals and fish can flourish.

• Understanding Water Quality: Water quality is paramount to a successful reef tank. Regular testing of parameters such as pH, ammonia, nitrites, and nitrates will help you maintain a healthy environment for all your tank's inhabitants.

• Marine Fish and Coral Care: The balance between fish, corals, and invertebrates is delicate. Understanding which species are compatible, how to acclimate them properly, and how to provide optimal care for each is crucial for long-term success.

• Sustainability: Eco-friendly practices, including using sustainable products, supporting coral farming, and adopting energy-efficient systems, are increasingly important as hobbyists aim to protect our natural reefs.

• Technology and Automation: As technology continues to evolve, reef keepers now have access to smart monitoring systems, automated equipment, and energy-efficient lighting that make reef keeping more manageable and enjoyable.

# MOVING FROM BEGINNER TO EXPERT REEF KEEPER

Becoming an expert reef keeper is a process that takes time, experience, and a willingness to adapt. As a beginner, focus on mastering the fundamentals: establishing a stable tank, understanding the needs of your fish and corals, and maintaining proper water quality. As you gain confidence, you can begin to experiment with more advanced techniques such as propagating corals, introducing more complex species, and utilizing automation to streamline tank maintenance.

The key to moving from beginner to expert is patience. Reef tanks evolve slowly, and each day brings new learning opportunities. The more time you spend observing your tank and troubleshooting issues, the better equipped you'll become to handle the complexities of advanced reef keeping.

# FINAL TIPS FOR SUCCESS IN YOUR REEF TANK JOURNEY

• Be Patient: Building a successful reef tank takes time. It's tempting to rush things, but let your tank mature and find its balance. Whether it's waiting for corals to grow or letting fish acclimate to their new home, patience is your best friend.

• Stay Educated: The world of reef keeping is constantly changing. New products, methods, and research continue to emerge. Stay informed by reading, engaging with the community, and learning from others' experiences.

• Observe and Adjust: Regular observation is crucial. Monitor the behavior of your fish, the health of your corals, and the water quality. If something isn't right, don't be afraid to make adjustments.

• Join the Community: The reef keeping community is full of passionate individuals willing to share their knowledge and experiences. Whether online or in person, connecting with fellow hobbyists can offer valuable insights and support.

• Keep It Fun: Above all, remember that reef keeping is a rewarding hobby. Don't let the challenges overwhelm you. Celebrate your successes, learn from your mistakes, and enjoy the beauty of your underwater world. With these tips and the knowledge you've gained, you're well on your way to becoming a successful reef keeper. Whether you're just starting your first reef tank or advancing to more complex systems, the journey is as rewarding as the destination. Happy reef keeping!

## Conclusion

As you dive into the captivating world of saltwater aquariums, you'll quickly realize that this hobby offers both challenges and immense rewards.

From the vibrant colors of your reef tank inhabitants to the tranquility of observing their interactions, reef keeping is an ongoing journey of discovery and growth.